Thomas Hodgkin

The Walls, Gates and Aqueducts of Rome

Thomas Hodgkin

The Walls, Gates and Aqueducts of Rome

ISBN/EAN: 9783744786607

Printed in Europe, USA, Canada, Australia, Japan

Cover: Foto ©Andreas Hilbeck / pixelio.de

More available books at **www.hansebooks.com**

THE WALLS, GATES

AND

AQUEDUCTS OF ROME.

By THOMAS HODGKIN, D.C.L.

LONDON:

JOHN MURRAY, ALBEMARLE STREET.

1899.

PREFACE.

The following extracts from the fourth volume of my "History of Italy and her Invaders," are made for the convenience of travellers who may desire to read on the spot the account there given of the Walls, Gates, and Aqueducts of Rome, but who could not easily find room in their baggage for a somewhat bulky volume.

The City of Rome was evacuated by the Ostrogoths, and entered by Belisarius, the general of Justinian, on the 9th of December, 536. Early in March, 537, the Ostrogothic host, under their King, Witigis, reappeared under its walls, and began the memorable siege which lasted for a year and nine days, but ended at last by their marching away, leaving the city untaken.

The story of that siege has been given us by the historian Procopius, a civil servant on the staff of Belisarius, and will be found transcribed at some length in the volume from which these extracts are taken. I refer to it now only in order to explain some allusions which might otherwise perplex the reader. I have reprinted here only so much of my book as describes the City (in the year 537), the Walls, and the Aqueducts of Rome.

THOMAS HODGKIN.

§ 1.—THE CITY OF ROME IN 536, AND THE WALLS OF AURELIUS AND HONORIUS.

536.
Belisarius fixes his quarters in the Pincian Palace.

Belisarius seems not to have taken up his abode in any of the imperial residences on the Palatine Hill, where the representative of the Byzantine Caesar might naturally have been expected to dwell, but, prescient of the coming struggle, to have at once fixed his quarters on the Pincian Hill. This ridge on the north of Rome, so well known by every visitor to the modern city, who, however short his stay, is sure to have seen the long train of carriages climbing to or returning from the fashionable drive, and who has probably stood upon its height in order to obtain the splendid view which it affords of the dome of St. Peter's, was not one of the original seven hills of the city, nor formed, strictly speaking, a part even of imperial Rome. Known in earlier times as the Collis Hortulorum, or Hill of Gardens, it occupied too commanding a position to be safely left outside the defences, and had therefore been included within the circuit of the walls of Honorius, some of the great retaining walls of the gardens of M. Q. Acilius Glabrio having been incorporated with the new defences[1]. Here then, in the Domus Pinciana[2], the imperial General took up his abode. Albeit probably somewhat dismantled, it was doubtless still a stately and spacious palace, though it has now disappeared and left no trace behind. It was admirably adapted for his purpose, being in fact a watch-tower commanding a view all round the

Advantages of the position.

---

[1] I give this fact on the authority of S. Lanciani, who considers this part of the wall to belong to the Republican age. Its comparatively early date is shown by the large masses of *opus reticulatum* which it contains, this diamond-shaped style of brickwork not having been used in Rome after the earliest age of the Empire.

[2] The Domus Pinciana is mentioned in Cassiodori Variarum, iii., 10, where Theodoric orders Festus to transport the marbles which it appears have been taken down from the Pincian house ('quae de domo Pinciana constat esse deposita') to Ravenna.

northern horizon, from the Vatican to the Mons Sacer[1]. From this point a ride of a few minutes on his swift charger would bring him to the next great vantage-ground, the Castra Praetoria, whose square enclosure, projecting beyond the ordinary line of the Honorian walls, made a tempting object of attack, but also a splendid watch-tower for defence, carrying on the general's view to the Praenestine Gate (Porta Maggiore) on the south-east of the city. Thus, from these two points, about a third of the whole circuit of the walls, and nearly all of that part which was actually attacked by the Goths, was visible.

That the city would have to be defended, and that it would tax all his powers to defend it successfully, was a matter that was perfectly clear to the mind of Belisarius, though the Romans, dwelling in a fool's paradise of false security, deemed that all their troubles were over when the 4000 Goths marched forth by the Flaminian Gate. They thought that the war would inevitably be decided elsewhere by some great pitched battle. It seemed to them obvious that so skilful a general as Belisarius would never consent to be besieged in a city so little defended by nature as was the wide circuit of imperial Rome, nor undertake the almost superhuman task of providing for the sustenance of that vast population in addition to his own army. Such, however, was the scheme of Belisarius, who knew that behind the walls of Rome his little army could offer a more effectual resistance to the enemy than in any pitched battle on the Campanian plains. Slowly and sadly the citizens awoke to the fact that their hasty defection from the Gothic cause was by no means to relieve them from the hardships of a siege. Possibly some of them, in the year of misery that lay before them, even envied the short and sharp agony of Neapolis.

The commissariat of the city was naturally one of the chief objects of the General's solicitude. From Sicily, still the granary of the State, his ships had brought and were daily bringing large supplies of grain. These were carried into the

---

[1] I think that this is correct, and probably an understatement of the extent of the view. But the groves and gardens of the Villas Borghese and Albani outside the walls make it difficult now to say exactly how much was visible from the Pincian in the time of Belisarius.

great warehouses (*horrea publica*), which were under the care of the Praefectus Annonae. At the same time the citizens, sorely grumbling, were set busily to work to bring into the city the corn and provisions of all kinds that were stored in the surrounding country. 536.

Repair of the walls.

Side by side with this great work went on the repair of the walls, which Belisarius found in many places somewhat ruinous. Two hundred and sixty years had elapsed since they were erected by Aurelian and Probus, one hundred and thirty since they were renewed by Honorius, and in the latter interval they may have suffered not only from the slow foot of time, but from the destroying hands of the soldiers of Alaric, of Gaiseric, and of Ricimer. Theodoric's steady and persevering labours had effected something, but much still remained to be done. Belisarius repaired the rents which still existed, drew a deep and wide fosse round the outer side of the wall, and supplied what he considered to be a deficiency in the battlements by adding a cross-wall to each on the left hand, so that the soldier might dispense with the use of a shield, being guarded against arrows and javelins hurled against him from that quarter [1].

Present aspect of these walls.

The walls and gates of imperial Rome, substantially the same walls which Belisarius defended, and many of the same gates at which the Goths battered, are still visible; and few historical monuments surpass them in interest. No survey of them has yet been made sufficiently minute to enable us to say with certainty to what date each portion of them belongs: but some general conclusions may be safely drawn even by the superficial observer. Here you may see the *opus reticulatum*, that cross-hatched brickwork which marks a building of the Julian or Flavian age; there the fine and regular brickwork of Aurelian; there again the poor debased work of the time of Honorius. A little further on, you come to a place where layers of bricks regularly laid cease altogether. Mere rubble-work thrust in anyhow, blocks of marble, fragments of columns; such is the material with which the fatal holes in the walls

[1] I presume that this is the meaning of Procopius. I am not able to state whether any traces of these cross-battlements or of the Belisarian fosse have been discovered.

have been darned and patched; and here antiquaries are generally disposed to see the 'tumultuary' restorations of Belisarius working in hot haste to complete his repairs before Witigis or the later Totila should appear before the walls. In a few places the gap in the brickwork is supplied by different and more massive materials. Great square blocks of the black volcanic stone called *tufa*, of which the wall of Servius Tullius was composed, are the sign of this intrusive formation. Are these also due to the rapid restorations of Belisarius, or was it part of the original plan to make the now superseded wall of the King do duty, after nine centuries, in the rampart of the Emperor? We turn an angle of the walls, and we see the mighty arches of the interlacing aqueducts by which Rome was fed with water from the Tiburtine and the Alban hills, with admirable skill made available for the defence of the city. We move onward, we come to Christian monograms, to mediaeval inscriptions, to the armorial bearings of Popes. At the south of the city we look upon the grand Bastion, which marks the restoring hand of the great Farnese Pope, Paul III, employing the genius of Sangallo. We pass the great gate of Ostia, that gate through which St. Paul is believed to have been led forth to martyrdom, and which now bears his name. The wall runs down sharply to the Tiber, at the foot of that strange artificial hill the Monte Testaccio; for half a mile it lines the left bank of the stream; then at the gate of Porto it reappears on the opposite side of the Tiber. Here it changes its character, and the change is itself a compendium of mediaeval history. The wall which on the eastern shore was Imperial, with only some marks of Papal repair, now becomes purely Papal; the turrets give place to bastions; Urban VIII, as name-giver to the rampart, takes the place of Aurelian[1]. We see at once how dear 'the Leonine city' was to the Pontifical heart; we discern that St. Peter's and the Vatican have taken the place which in Imperial Rome was occupied by the Palatine, in Republican Rome by the Forum, the Capitol, and the Temple of Concord.

---

[1] The course of the wall of Aurelian is indeed visible in many places in the Trans-tiberine region, but it is merely an archaeological curiosity there, quite eclipsed in importance by the Papal fortification.

As everywhere in Rome, so pre-eminently in our circuit of *53G. Contrasted periods of history.* the wall, the oldest and the newest ages are constantly jostling against one another. At the east of the city we were looking at the tufa blocks hewn by the masons of Servius Tullius. Now on the west we see the walls by the Porta Aurelia showing everywhere the dints of French bullets hurled against them when Oudinot in 1849 crushed out the little life of the Roman Republic of Mazzini. For yet more recent history we turn again to our northern starting-point, and there, almost under the palace of Belisarius, we see the stretch of absolutely new wall which marks the extent of the practicable breach through which the troops of Victor Emmanuel entered Rome in September, 1870.

A first and even a second perambulation of the walls of *Object of Aurelian in building the walls.* Rome, especially on the outside, may hardly give the observer an adequate conception of their original completeness as a work of defence. It has been well pointed out by one of our German authorities[1] that Aurelian's object in constructing it cannot have been merely to furnish cover for the comparatively small numbers of the *cohortes urbanae*, the ordinary city-guard, but that he must have contemplated the necessity of a whole army garrisoning the city and defending his work. For this reason we have in Aurelian's original line of circumvallation, and to some extent, but less perfectly, in the Honorian *The inner gallery.* restoration of it, a complete gallery or covered way carried all round the inside of the wall[2]. Nowhere can this original idea of the wall be better studied than on the south-east of the city, in the portion between the Amphitheatrum Castrense and the Porta Asinaria, or, in ecclesiastical language, between the Church of Santa Croce and that of St. John Lateran. Here, if we walk outside, we see the kind of work with which the rest of our tour of inspection has already made us familiar, that is, a wall from 50 to 60 feet high, with square towers some 20 feet higher than the rest of the work, projecting from the circuit of

[1] Jordan, Topographie der Stadt Rom, i. 348.

[2] In the works erected at Chollerford in Northumberland (Cilurnum), for the defence of the bridge over the North Tyne, we find a humbler specimen of the same kind of covered way.

536.   the wall at regular intervals of 33 yards [1]. If we now pass in, not by the Porta Asinaria, which is closed, but by its representative the modern Porta San Giovanni, we find ourselves looking upon a structure greatly resembling one of the great Roman aqueducts, and probably often taken for such by travellers. We can see of course the backs of the square towers, but between every two of these there are seven tall arches about 33 feet high. A window through the wall near the bottom of each of these corresponds with an opening outside about half-way up the face of the wall, and thus lets us see that the level of the ground inside is from 20 to 30 feet higher than outside, the apparent height of the wall inside being of course reduced by the same amount. In the wall behind the arches we can see the holes marking the places where the ends of two sets of rafters, one above the other, have rested. Moreover, the piers which separate the arches are pierced by another set of tall thin arches at right angles to the others. The meaning of all these indications evidently is that a corridor or covered way round the whole inner circuit of the wall of Aurelian, where that was finished according to the design of the imperial builder. This gallery was two stories high between the towers; a third story would be added where these gave the needful height [2]. Besides these covered galleries, which were used for the rapid transfer of troops from one part of the circuit

---

[1] Exactly 100 Roman feet. The face of the tower (C D) is 24 feet long, the sides (B C, D E) 12 feet.

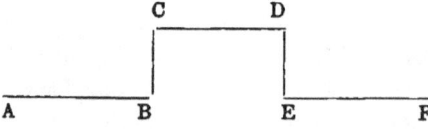

Many maps of modern Rome indicate the presence of these square towers. The greater or less regularity of their occurrence is generally a safe indication of the better or worse preservation of the original wall.

[2] In the corridor on the western side of the Porta S. Sebastiano, at the third tower from the gate, Mr. Parker discovered an early fresco representing the Virgin with the infant Christ, which he believes to be 'the earliest Madonna that is known as distinct from the offering of the Magi.' Whether his inference that a chapel was constructed here for the soldiers at the time of Theodoric's repairs be correct or not, at any rate the existence of the fresco is an interesting fact (Archaeology of Rome, i. 168).

536.

to another, there was the regular path at the top of the walls, partially protected by battlements, on which the defenders were doubtless mustered when actual fighting was going forward.

For our knowledge of the fortifications of the city we are not entirely dependent on our present observation of the walls, battered as they have been by the storms of the Middle Ages, and still more grievously as they have suffered at the hands of restorers and modernisers in the last three centuries. The 'Pilgrim of Einsiedeln,' as he is conventionally termed, a visitor to Rome in the eighth or ninth century, recorded the most noteworthy objects of the Eternal City in a MS. which is preserved in the monastery of Einsiedeln in Switzerland. Among other information, he gives us the precise number of the towers, the battlements, and the loopholes in each section of the wall, including even the sanitary arrangements rendered necessary by the permanent presence of a large body of troops. It has been generally supposed that the Einsiedeln Pilgrim himself counted the towers of the sacred city of St. Peter ; but the previously mentioned German authority [1] suggests, with great probability, that he is really transcribing some much earlier official document, possibly that drawn up by the architects of Honorius at the beginning of the fifth century [2].

While Belisarius is repairing the mouldering walls and assigning to the rude cohorts of his many-nationed army their various duties in the anticipated siege, we may allow ourselves to cast a hasty glance over the city which he has set himself to defend. A hasty glance, for this is not the time nor the place for minute antiquarian discussion ; yet a glance of some sad and earnest interest, since we know that

State of the walls in the eighth century.

The Pilgrim of Einsiedeln

General survey of Rome before the siege.

---

[1] Jordan, Topographie der Stadt Rom, ii. 156, 170. He suggests ' Ammon the geometer,' who, according to Olympiodorus (apud Photium, Bonn edition, p. 469), ' took the measure of the walls of Rome at the time when the Goths made their attack upon the city.'

[2] The reader may be interested in seeing this technical description of that portion of the defences which was chiefly conspicuous in the Gothic siege of Rome. The *turres* and *fenestrae* (towers and loopholes) need no explanation : the *propugnacula* are the battlements, or to speak more

536.

this is the last time that Rome in her glory will be seen by
mortal man. The things which have befallen her up to
this time have been only slight and transitory shocks, which
have left no lasting dint upon her armour—Alaric's burning
of the palace of Sallust, Gaiseric's half-accomplished spoliation
of the golden roof of the temple of Jupiter Capitolinus, some
havoc wrought in the insolence of their triumph by the
foederati of Ricimer. More destructive, no doubt, was the
slow process of denudation already commenced by the
unpatriotic hands of the Romans themselves, and only
partially checked by the decrees of Majorian and Theodoric.
Still, as a whole, Rome the Golden City, the City of
Consuls and Emperors, the City of Cicero's orations, of
Horace's idle perambulations, of Trajan's magnificent con-
structions, yet stood when the Gothic war began. In the
squalid, battered, depopulated cluster of ruins, over which
twenty-eight years later sounded the heralds' trumpets
proclaiming that the Gothic war was ended, it would have
been hard for Cicero, Horace, or Trajan to recognise his home.
Classical Rome we are looking on for the last time ; the Rome
of the Middle Ages, the city of sacred shrines and relics
and pilgrimages, is about to take her place.

accurately, the merlons of the embattled wall ; *necessariae* are believed to
be equivalent to latrinae. It will be remembered that 100 Roman feet
was the regulation distance between tower and tower.
'A portâ Flamineâ cum ipsâ portâ usque ad portam Pincianam
clausam:
Turres xxviii, propugnacula dcxliiii, necessariae iii, fenestrae majores
forinsecus lxxv, minores cxvii.
A portâ Pincianâ clausâ cum ipsâ portâ usque ad portam Salariam :
Turrs xxii, ppg ccxlvi, necess xvii, fenest. major forins cc, minor clx.
A portâ Salariâ cum ipsâ portâ usque Numentanam :
Turr x. ppg cxcviiii, nec ii, fen major forins lxxi, min lxv.
A portâ Numentanâ cum ipsâ portâ usque Tiburtinam :
Turr lvii, ppg, dcccvi, necess ii, fen major forins ccxiiii, minor cc.
A portâ Tiburtinâ cum ipsâ portâ usque ad Praenestinam :
Turr xviiii, ppg cum portâ Praenestinâ cccii, necess i, fen major forins
lxxx, minor cviii.
A portâ Praenestinâ usque ad Asinariam :
Turr xxvi, ppg diiii, nec vi, fenst major forins clxxx, minor cl.
A portâ Asinariâ usque Metroviam :
Turr xx, ppg cccxlii, nec iiii, fenest major forins cxxx, minor clxxx.'
(From Jordan's Topographie der Stadt Rom, ii. 578-9.)

536.
Silence of
Procopius
as to the
effect pro-
duced on
him by the
sight of
Rome.

It is impossible not to regret that Procopius has allowed himself to say so little as to the impression made on him by Rome. He must have entered the city soon after his chief, travelling by the Appian Way, the smooth and durable construction of which moved him to great admiration [1]. But of the city itself, except of its gates and walls in so far as these require description in order to illustrate the siege, he has very little to say. It is easy to understand his silence. Most authors shrink from writing about the obvious and well-known. It would perhaps be easier to meet with ten vivid descriptions of the Island of Skye than one of the Strand or Cheapside. But not the less is it a loss for us that this quick and accurate observer, the Herodotus of the Post-Christian age, has not recorded more of his impressions of the streets, the buildings, and the people of Rome. Let us endeavour, however, to put ourselves in his place, and to reconstruct the city, at least in general outline, as he must have beheld it.

Imaginary
progress of
Procopius
through the
city.

Porta Appia.

Journeying, as it is most probable that Procopius did, by the Appian Way, he would enter Rome by the gate then called the Porta Appia, but now the Porta di San Sebastiano, one of the finest of the still remaining entrances through the wall of Aurelian, with two noble towers, square within and semi-circular without, the upper part of which, according to a careful English observer [2], bears traces of the restoring hand of Theo-

*

[1] These are his words (De B. G. i. 14) : 'Now the Via Appia is a five days' journey for a good pedestrian, leading from Rome to Capua. It is so broad that two waggons can pass one another along its whole course, and it is eminently worthy of observation. For all the stones composing it being mill-stones and very hard by nature were brought by Appius from quarries a long way off, there being none like them in the district itself. Having made these stones smooth and even and cut them into polygons, they fitted them one into another without using rubble or any other cement. Now these stones cohere so perfectly with one another that they look as if they had not been artificially joined but had grown together. Nor has their smoothness been impaired by the daily passage of horses and waggons over them for so great a length of time. They still fit as perfectly as ever and have lost nothing of their original beauty.' (Chalica, 'rubble or cement,' is Comparetti's conjectural emendation for Chalca, 'brass.')

[2] Mr. J. H. Parker.

536.

doric [1]. Immediately after entering the city, Procopius would find himself passing under the still-preserved Arch of Drusus; and those of Trajan and Verus, spanning the intra-mural portion of the Appian Way, would before long attract his notice. This portion of the city, now so desolate and empty of inhabitants, was then probably thickly sown with the houses of the lower order of citizens.

The Baths of Caracalla.

High on his left, when he had proceeded somewhat more than half-a-mile, rose the mighty pile known to the ancients as the Thermae Antoninianae, and to the moderns as the Baths of Caracalla. Even in its ruins this building gives to the spectator an almost overwhelming idea of vastness and solidity. But when Procopius first saw it, the 1600 marble seats for bathers [2] were probably all occupied, the gigantic swimming-bath was filled with clear cold water from the Marcian aqueduct, the great circular *Caldarium*, 160 feet in diameter, showed dimly through the steam the forms of hundreds of bathing Romans. Men were wrestling in the Palaestra and walking up and down in the Peristyle connected with the baths. Polished marble and deftly wrought mosaics lined the walls and covered the floors. At every turn one came upon some priceless work of art, like the Farnese Bull, the Hercules, the Flora, those statues the remnants of which, dug out of these ruins as from an unfailing quarry, have immortalised the names of Papal Nephews and made the fortunes of the museums of Bourbon Kings [3].

The buildings on the Palatine.

And now, as the traveller moved on, there rose more and more proudly above him the hill which has become for all later ages synonymous with regal power and magnificence, the imperial Palatine. Not as now, with only a villa and a convent

---

[1] A curious inscription on the left-hand wall inside this gate (accompanied by the figure of an archangel) records the invasion of *gens foresteria* on the last day but one before the feast of St. Michael, and their 'abolition' by the Roman people under the command of Jacobus de Pontianis. The *gens foresteria* were the troops of King Robert of Naples co-operating with the Orsini, in the year 1327.

[2] Olympiodorus apud Photium, p. 469 (ed. Bonn).

[3] The first impression of a visitor to the Museums of Sculpture at Rome and Naples is that every important work came either from the Baths of Caracalla or from the Villa of Hadrian.

standing erect upon it. the rest, grass and wild-flowers, and ruins for the most part not rising above the level of the ground. The whole hill was crowded with vast palaces, in which each successive dynasty had endeavoured to outshine its predecessor in magnificence. Here, first, rose the tall but perhaps some-what barbarous edifice with which Severus had determined to arrest the attention of his fellow-provincials from Africa travelling along the Appian Way, in order that their first question about Rome might be answered by his name. Just below it was the mysterious Septizonium, the work of the same Emperor, the porch of his palace and the counterpart of his tomb, of whose seven sets of columns, rising tier above tier, three were yet remaining only three centuries ago, when the remorseless Sixtus V transported them to the Vatican. Behind the palace of Severus, on the summit of the Palatine, were visible the immense banqueting halls of the Flavian Emperors, Vespasian and Domitian; behind them again the more modest house of Tiberius, and the labyrinth of apart-ments reared by the crazy Caligula.

In what condition are we to suppose that all these imperial dwellings were maintained when the troops of the Eastern Caesar came to reclaim them for their lord? Certainly not with all that untarnished magnificence which they possessed before the troubles of the third century commenced; hardly even with the show of affluence which they may still have worn when Constantius visited Rome in 357. Two centuries had elapsed since then—two centuries of more evil than good fortune— centuries in which the struggle for mere existence had left the rulers of the State little money or time to spare for repairs or decorations. But nothing, it may fairly be argued, had yet occurred to bring these massive piles into an obviously ruinous condition. If the comparison may be allowed, these dwellings on the Palatine probably presented in the state apartments that dingy appearance of faded greatness which one sees in the country-house of a noble family long resident abroad, but externally they had lost nothing of the stateliness with which they were meant to impress the mind of the beholder.

If Procopius ascended to the summit of the Palatine he may perchance have seen from thence, in the valley of the Circus

536.

Probable condition of the imperial palaces.

Circus Maximus.

536.

Maximus, between the Palatine and Aventine hills, a chariot-race exhibited by the General to keep the populace in good-humour. Here the Byzantine official would feel himself to be at once at home. Whether he favoured the Blue or the Green faction we know not (though his animosity against Theodora makes us incline to suspect him of sympathy with the Greens), but to whichsoever he belonged he could see his own faction striving for victory, and would hear, from at any rate a large portion of the crowd, the shouts with which they hailed the triumph, or the groans with which they lamented the defeat, of their favourite colour.

Arch of Constantine.

Continuing his journey, the historian passed under the eastern summit of the Palatine, and then beneath the Arch of Constantine, that Arch which stands at this day comparatively undefaced, showing how the first Christian emperor purloined the work of the holier heathen Trajan to commemorate his own less worthy victories. Emerging from the shadow of the Arch, he stood before the Flavian Amphitheatre and looked up to the immense Colossus of Nero, that statue of the Sun-god 120 feet in height, towering almost as high as the mighty edifice itself, to which it gave its best-known name, the Colosseum. It is generally felt that the Colosseum is one of those buildings which has gained by ruin. The topmost story, consisting, not of arches like the three below it, but of mere blank wall-spaces divided by pilasters, must have had when unbroken a somewhat heavy appearance ; while, on the other hand, no beholder of the still perfect building could derive that impression of massive strength which we gain by looking, through the very chasms and rents in its outer shell, at the gigantic circuit of its concentric ellipses, at the massive walls radiating upwards and outwards upon which the seats of its 87,000 spectators rested. Altogether there is a pathetic majesty in the ruined Colosseum which can hardly have belonged to it in its days of prosperity, and, as one is almost inclined to say, of vulgar self-assertion [1].

The Colosseum and the Colossus.

But if this be true of the Colosseum itself, it is not true of the surrounding objects. The great Colossus has already

---

[1] This remark is made in Burn's Old Rome. p. 71.

been referred to. It is now represented only by a shapeless and unsightly heap of stones which once formed part of its pedestal. The ugly conical mass of brickwork near the same spot, and known as the Meta Sudans, was a beautiful upspringing fountain thirty or forty feet high when Procopius passed that way.

Eastwards, on the Oppian hill, stretched the long line of the Thermae Titi, the baths reared by Titus above the vast ruins of the Golden House of Nero. Immediately in front of the Colosseum (on the north-west) was the double temple reared by Hadrian in honour of Venus and Rome[1], perhaps one of the most beautiful edifices in the whole enclosure of the city. It was composed of two temples placed back to back. In one was the statue of Venus the Prosperous (Venus Felix), looking towards the Colosseum, in the other *Roma Aeterna* sat gazing towards her own Capitol. In the curvilinear pediment of the latter was a frieze, according to the opinion of some archaeologists representing Mars caressing Rhea Sylvia, and the wolf suckling their heroic offspring. Around the whole structure ran a low colonnade containing four hundred pillars.

The famous Sacred Way, where once Horace loitered, a well-marked street, not as now a mere track through the midst of desolation, led the historian up to the marble arch of Titus. Here he doubtless looked, as we may yet look, upon the representation of the seven-branched candlestick and the other spoils of Jerusalem, the strange story of whose wanderings he has himself recorded for us in his history of the Vandalic War[2].

Descending the slope of the Via Sacra, and having on his right the lofty Basilica of Constantine, whose gigantic arches

Margin notes: 536. Meta Sudans. The Baths of Titus. Temple of Venus and Rome. The Via Sacra. Arch of Titus. Basilica of Constantine.

[1] This was the Temple which according to Dion Cassius cost the architect Apollodorus his life. Hadrian sent him a drawing of the Temple which he had himself designed, expecting a compliment on his artistic skill, and received for answer, 'You have made your goddesses so large that they cannot stand up in their own houses,' a criticism in return for which Hadrian is said to have put him to death (lxix. 4).

[2] ii. 9. See Vol. II. p. 286, and Vol. III. p. 694. (625 2nd ed.)

(long but erroneously called the Temple of Peace) stand on
their hill over against the Palatine, and seem to assert a
predominance over its yet remaining ruins, Procopius now
with each downward step saw the glories of the Roman

Forum more fully revealed. On his left, the temple of the
Great Twin Brethren, three of whose graceful Corinthian
columns still survive, a well-known object to all visitors to the
Forum.   Hard by, the fountain from which the celestial horse-
men gave their horses to drink after the battle of Lake
Regillus.   Further on, the long colonnades of the Basilica of
Julius, four law-courts under the same roof.   On his right, the
tall columns of the Temple of Antoninus and Faustina, perhaps
already supporting the roof of a Christian shrine, though not
the unsightly edifice which at present clings to and defaces
them ; the chapel of the great Julius, the magnificent Basilica
of Aemilius ; and, lastly, those two venerable objects, centres
for so many ages of all the political life of Rome, the Senate-
house and the Rostra.   The Senate was still a living body,
though its limbs had long been shaken by the palsies of
a timid old age ; but the days when impassioned orators
thundered to the Roman people from the lofty Rostra had
long passed away.   Yet we may be permitted to conjecture that
Procopius, with that awe-struck admiration which he had for
'the Romans of old time,' gazed upon those weathern-worn
trophies of the sea and mused on the strange contradictoriness
of Fate, which had used all the harangues of those impetuous
orators as instruments to fashion the serene and silent despotism
of Justinian.

At the end of the Forum, with an embarrassment of
wealth which perplexes us even in their ruins, rise the Arch
of Septimius Severus, the Temple of Concord, the Temple of
Vespasian, the ill-restored Temple of Saturn.   Between them
penetrated the Clivus Capitolinus, up which once slowly
mounted the car of many a triumphant general.   Behind all
stretched the magnificent background of the Capitoline Hill, on
the left-hand summit of which stood the superb mass of the
Temple of Jupiter Capitolinus, robbed by Gaiseric of half its
golden tiles, but still resplendent under the western sun.   Then
came the saddle-shaped depression faced by the long Tabularium :

and then the right-hand summit of the Capitoline, crowned by the Temple of Juno Moneta [1].

We have supposed our historian to deviate a little from the straight path in order to explore to the uttermost the buildings of the Republican Forum; but as his business lies at the northern extremity of the city, he must retrace a few of his steps and avail himself of the line of communication between the Via Sacra and the Via Flaminia which was opened up by the beneficent despotism of the Emperors. That is to say, he must leave the Forum of the Republic and traverse the long line of the spacious and well-planned Fora of the Caesars. In no part is the contrast between ancient and modern Rome more humiliating than here. In our day, a complex of mean and irregular streets [2], almost entirely destitute of classical interest or mediaeval picturesqueness, fills up the interval between the Capitoline and the Quirinal hills. The deeply cut entablature of the Temple of Minerva resting upon the two half-buried 'Colonnacce' in front of the baker's shop, the three pillars of the Temple of Mars Ultor, the great feudal fortress of the Tor de' Conti, and that most precious historical monument the Column of Trajan, alone redeem this region from utter wearisomeness. But this space, now so crowded and so irregular, was once the finest bit of architectural landscape-gardening in Rome. The Forum of Vespasian, the Forum of Nerva, the Forum of Augustus, the Forum of Julius, the Forum of Trajan, a series of magnificent squares and arcades, opening one into the other, occupying a space some 600 yards long by 100 wide and terminating in the mighty granite pillars of the Temple of Trajan, produced on the mind of the beholder the same kind of effect, but on a far grander scale, which is wrought by Trafalgar Square in London or the Place de la Concorde in Paris. Let not the modern traveller, who, passing from the Corso to the Colosseum, is accosted by his driver with

---

[1] A long and bitter controversy is at length put to rest by the attribution of the Temple of Jupiter Capitolinus to the height now occupied by the Palazzo Caffarelli, and by placing the Arx where now stands the Church of Ara Coeli.

[2] Via Bonella, Via Alessandrina, and so forth.

536.

the glibly uttered words 'Foro Trajano,' suppose that the little oblong space with a few pillar-bases, which he beholds at the foot of the memorable Column, is indeed even in ruin the entire Forum of the greatest of the Emperors. The column is Trajan's column doubtless, though

'Apostolic statues climb
To crush the imperial urn whose ashes slept sublime
Buried in air, the deep blue sky of Rome,
And looking to the stars.'

The Forum of Trajan.

But the so-called 'Foro Trajano' is only a small transverse section of one member of the Trajanic series, the Basilica Ulpia. The column, as is well known, measured the height of earth which had to be dug away from a spur of the Capitoline hill in order to form the Forum. Between it and the Basilica Ulpia rose the two celebrated libraries of Greek and Latin authors, and between these two buildings stood once, and probably yet stood in the days of Procopius, that 'everlasting statue' of brass which by the Senate's orders was erected in honour of Sidonius, Poet-laureate and son-in-law of an Emperor [1].

The Libraries

In those Libraries Procopius, in the intervals of the business and peril of the siege, may often have wandered in order to increase his acquaintance with the doings of 'the Romans of old.' What treasures of knowledge, now for ever lost to the world, were still enshrined in those apartments! There all the rays of classical Art and Science were gathered into a focus. More important perhaps for us, all that the Greeks and Romans knew (and it was not a little, though carelessly recorded) concerning the Oriental civilisation which preceded theirs, and concerning the Teutonic barbarism which encompassed it, was still contained in those magnificent literary collections. There was the Chaldaean history of Berosus, there were the authentic Egyptian king-lists of Manetho, there was Livy's story of the last days of the Republic and the first days of the Empire, there was Tacitus's full history of the conquest of Britain, all that Ammianus could tell about the troubles of the third century and the conversion of Constantine, all that Cassiodorus had written about the royal Annals and the dim original of the

[1] See vol. ii. p. 390 (388 2nd ed.)

Goths. All this perished, apparently in those twenty years of desolating war which now lie before us. It may be doubted whether for us the loss of the Bibliothecae Ulpiae is not even more to be regretted than that of the Library of Alexandria [1].

Ammianus tells us [2] that when the Emperor Constantius visited Rome he gazed with admiration on the Capitol, the Colosseum, the Pantheon, and the Theatre of Pompey, but still with admiration which could express itself in words. 'But when,' says the historian, 'he came to the Forum of Trajan, that structure unique in all the world, and, as I cannot but think, marvellous in the eyes of the Divinity himself, he beheld with silent amazement those gigantic interlacings of stones which it is past the power of speech to describe, and which no mortal must in future hope to imitate. Hopeless of ever attempting any such work himself, he would only look at the horse of Trajan, placed in the middle of the vestibule [3] and bearing the statue of the Emperor. "That," said Constantius, "I can imitate, and I will." Hormisdas, a royal refugee from the court of Persia, replied, with his nation's quickness of repartee, "But first, O Emperor, if you can do so, order a stable to be built as fair as that before us, that your horse may have as fine an exercising ground as the one we are now looking upon." '

Emerging from the imperial Fora, Procopius would now enter upon the Via Lata, broad as its name denotes, one of the longest streets, if not the longest, in Rome, and very nearly corresponding to the modern Corso. The Subura, which lay a little to the east of the Forum of Augustus, was once at any

---

[1] The words of Vopiscus (Vita Probi, II), ' Usus sum praecipue libris ex Bibliotheca Ulpia, *aetate mea thermis Diocletianis*,' have been interpreted as meaning that all the contents of Trajan's libraries had been transported to the Baths of Diocletian. I think, however, we may fairly infer from Sidonius's verses about his statue,

' Inter auctores utriusque fixam
Bibliothecae,'

either that this removal had been only partial, or that at some time between 300 and 450 the books had been brought back to their original home.

[2] xvi. 10. 15.   [3] Atrium.

536.

rate one of the most thickly peopled districts of Rome, and we shall perhaps not be wrong in assuming that in the regions east of the Via Lata, upon the Quirinal, Viminal, and Esquiline Hills, where the tall buildings of the Fourth Rome, the Rome of Victor Emmanuel and United Italy, are now arising, the humbler classes of the Second or Imperial Rome had chiefly fixed their abodes.

On the left side of the Via Lata, where the Third or Papal Rome has spun its web of streets thickest, all or nearly all was yet given up to pleasure. This was the true West End of Rome, the region in which her parks and theatres were chiefly placed. Here were the great open spaces of the Campus Martius and Campus Flaminius; here two race-courses, those of Flaminius and Domitian; here the great theatres of Pompey, of Balbus, and of Marcellus, and the Porticoes of the Argonauts and of Octavia. Altogether it was a region devoted to pleasure and idleness by the side of the tawny Tiber, and most unlike the closely-built and somewhat dingy quarters of the city which now occupy it.

Campus Martius, circuses, and theatres west of the Via Lata.

As Procopius moved along the straight course of the Via Lata his eye would probably be caught by the flat dome of the Pantheon, hovering over the buildings on his left [1]. He would thread the Arch of Claudius, would stand at the foot of the Column of Marcus Aurelius, and then pass beneath that Emperor's Arch of Triumph. Two mighty sepulchres would then arrest his attention : the Tomb of Hadrian [2] seeming by its massive bulk almost close at hand, though on the other bank of the Tiber ; and the Mausoleum of Augustus rising immediately on his left, a rotunda of white marble below, a green and shady pleasaunce above, recalling, by its wonderful admixture of Nature and Art, the far-famed Hanging Gardens of Babylon.

Pantheon.

Tomb of Hadrian.

Mausoleum of Augustus.

And now at length his never-to-be-forgotten first view of Rome was drawing to a close. The soon-sinking sun of late autumn warned him, perchance, to quicken his pace. He bore off to the right : by some steep steps where the receivers of the

---

[1] 'Pantheum velut regionem teretem speciosa celsitudine fornicatam' (Ammianus, xvi. 10. 14).

[2] Now the Castle of S. Angelo.

public alimony[1] were wont to cluster, he climbed the high   536.
garden-decked Pincian. He entered the palace, bowed low
before Belisarius, lower yet before the imperious Antonina, and
received the General's orders as to the share of work that he
was to undertake in connection with the provisionment of the
city. Such is an account, imaginary indeed, but not improbable,
of the circumstances in which the soldier-secretary first entered
and first beheld Rome reunited to the Roman Empire.

It remains for us briefly to notice the rising importance of
the Christian buildings of Rome, though we will here dispense
with the imaginary companionship of Procopius, whose some-   Christian buildings of Rome.
what sceptical temper, 'well acquainted with the subjects in
dispute among Christians, but determined to say as little as
possible about them, holding it to be proof of a madman's
folly to enquire into the nature of God,' would make him an
uncongenial guest at the sacred shrines. Of the five great
patriarchal churches of Rome, three were beyond the walls of
the city. On its extreme verge stood what was still the
foremost in dignity of all the five, St. John Lateran, or
the Basilica of Canstantine, the so-called Mother-Church of
Christendom, ' Omnium Urbis et Orbis Ecclesiarum Caput.'
It stood near the Asinarian Gate, on the property which Fausta,   Basilica of Constantine: St. John Lateran.
the unhappy wife of Constantine, inherited from her father
Maximian, and which had once belonged to the senatorial
family of the Laterani ; and it formed the subject of that real
and considerable donation of the first Christian Emperor to the
Bishops of Rome which later ages distorted into a quasi-feudal
investiture of the Imperial City.

Upon the Vatican Hill, outside the walls of Aurelian, looking
down upon the Tiber and the Tomb of Hadrian, rose the five
long aisles, the semicircular apse, and the nearly square   Vatican Basilica: St. Peter's.
entrance-Atrium of the Basilica of St. Peter. The region
immediately surrounding it was perhaps still called the Gardens
of Nero. It is certain that the reason for placing the Basilica
on that spot was that there was the traditional site of the
martyrdom of the Apostle, as well as of the sufferings of the

[1] *Panis gradilis.*

536.

nameless Christian crowd who, dressed in cloaks covered with pitch and set on fire, served as living torches to light that throned Satan to his revels and his chariot-races on the Vatican-mount.

St. Paul's

Outside the gate of Ostia, and also near the traditional scene of the martyrdom of the Apostle to whom it was dedicated, stood the noble Basilica of St. Paul. This edifice, which was commenced by Theodosius, completed by Honorius, and received the finishing touches to its decorations at the hand of Placidia under the guidance of Pope Leo[1], subsisted with but little change to the days of our fathers. The lamentable fire of 1823, by which the greater part of it was destroyed, took from us the most interesting relic of Christian Imperial Rome. Happily the restoration, though it cannot give us back the undiminished interest of the earlier building, has been executed with admirable fidelity to the original design.

Liberian Basilica : Sta. Maria Maggiore.

This cannot be said of the Liberian Basilica, the great church now known as S. Maria Maggiore, which, standing high on the Esquiline Hill, looked down westwards on the crowded Subura, and northwards towards the palatial Baths of Diocletian. The outside of the building has sustained the extremity of insult and wrong at the hands of the tasteless pseudo-classical restorers of the eighteenth century ; and the inside, though not absolutely ruined by them, though its mosaics are still visible and much of its long colonnade still remains, shows too plainly how unsafe were the treasures of Christian antiquity in the hands of the conceited architects of the Renaissance.

St. Lawrence.

The last of the great Basilicas, that of the martyred St. Lawrence, one mile outside the Tiburtine Gate, has suffered less ravage at the hands of restorers. It was in the thirteenth century singularly re-arranged and transformed, its apse being pulled down and turned into a nave, and its original vestibule being turned into a choir[2] : still we have substantially before

---

[1] ' Placidiae pia mens operis decus /homne (sic) paterni
Gaudet pontificis studio splendere Leonis.'
(Inscription over the arch in S. Paolo fuori le Mura.)

[2] See Freeman's Historical and Architectural Sketches, 213-215, for an account of these transformations.

us the same church which was surrounded by the Gothic armies in their siege of Rome. With that blending of the old and of the very new which at once charms and bewilders the visitor to Rome, we have here again an inscription recording the work of 'the pious mind of Placidia' under the guidance of Attila's Pope Leo, and in the crypt the just erected tomb of Pio Nono. The latter is so placed as to command a view of the slab of marble dyed red with the blood of the deacon Laurentius, martyr for the faith under the Emperor Claudius Gothicus. This marble slab was a favourite relic with the late Pontiff.

Besides these five great patriarchal churches there were *The parish churches,* twenty-eight parish churches, known by the technical name of *or Tituli.* *Tituli,* from which the Cardinal-presbyters of a later age took their ecclesiastical designations [1]. Some of these which have been preserved to this day are more interesting than the churches of greater dignity, having by reason of their comparative insignificance escaped the hand of the Renaissance destroyer [2].

The main features, which were evidently common to all the *Chief features* Christian edifices of Rome in the fifth and sixth centuries, *of the ecclesiastical architecture* were (1) a long line of columns, not by any means always *of the fifth and sixth* uniform or of the same order of architecture, and generally *centuries.* taken from the outside of some heathen temple ; (2) a semi-circular apse at the eastern end, in which the bishop or presbyter sat surrounded by his inferior clergy, as the Roman magistrate in the original Basilica sat surrounded by the various members of his 'officium' ; (3) an arch in front of the apse, the idea of which was probably borrowed from the triumphal arches of the Emperors ; (4) upon the arch, upon the apse, on the flat wall-space above the arches, in fact wherever they could conveniently be introduced, a blaze of bright mosaics, like those still preserved to us at Ravenna and in a very few of these Roman churches. The subjects represented were the Saviour, the symbols of the four Evangelists, the twelve Apostles under the guise of sheep, the mystic cities

[1] See a very complete list of the Tituli in Gregorovius, i. 251-259.

[2] Such are Santa Prassede, San Clemente, and Santa Agnese.

536.

Jerusalem and Bethlehem, the Jordan and the four rivers of Paradise, and other emblems of the same character.

The fact that the columns of these churches were as a rule taken from heathen temples must of course qualify to some extent the statement that the splendour of the city was undiminished when Procopius entered it. Temples, not merely abandoned to silence and solitude, but rudely stripped of their pillared magnificence, must in many places have offended the eye of a beholder more sensitive to beauty than to religious enthusiasm. Still upon the whole, and with this abatement, we may repeat our proposition that it was the stately Rome of Consuls and Emperors which men then looked upon, and which after the middle of the sixth century they never beheld again.

'Alas, for Earth, for never shall we see
That brightness in her eye she bore when Rome was free.'

* * * * * * * * *

537.
The Siege
of Rome
begun.

About three months after the entry of Belisarius began the First Siege of Rome by the Ostrogoths, the longest and one of the deadliest that the Eternal City has ever endured. It began in the early days of March 537, and was not to end till a year and nine days later in the March of 538[1]. When morning dawned, the Goths, who entertained no doubt of an early success against so large and helpless a city, proceeded to intrench themselves in seven camps, six on the eastern and one on the western side of the Tiber. They did not thus accomplish a perfect blockade of the city, but they did obstruct, in a tolerably effectual manner, eight out of its fourteen gates. As

[1] Lord Mahon (Earl Stanhope), in his Life of Belisarius (p. 246), endeavours to fix the date of the beginning of the siege to March 12. He does this by assigning the vernal equinox (March 21) for its close. The words of Procopius, however (ii. 186, ed. Bonn), seem to me too vague to support this exact conclusion: and, on the other hand, his statement that it began 'at the outset of March' (p. 117), coupled with the general course of the narrative which describes a large number of events before 'the winter ended and the second year of the war' (p. 154), indicates a very early date in March for the beginning of the siege. It does not seem possible to define it more accurately than this.

frequent reference in the course of this history will be made to one or other of these gates, it will be well to give a list of them here, with their ancient and modern names, printing those that were obstructed by the Goths in italics.

To give some idea of the distance of one gate from another the number of square towers between each pair of gates is added on the authority of the Pilgrim of Einsiedeln. The intervals between the towers varied from 100 to 300 and even 400 feet, the wider spaces being chiefly found on the west side of the Tiber.

Ancient Name.	Modern Name.	No. of Towers.
East bank of the Tiber:—		
1. *Porta Flaminia*	*P. del Popolo.*	51.
2. *Porta Salaria*	*P. Salara.*	10.
3. *Porta Nomentana* near to	*P. Pia.*	57.
4. *Porta Tiburtina* . . .	*P. San Lorenzo.*	19.
5. *Porta Praenestina &)*	*P. Maggiore.*	
6. *Porta Labicana)*		26.
7. Porta Asinaria . near to	P. San Giovanni.	20.
8. Porta Metrovia (or Metronia)	Closed.	20
9. Porta Latina	Closed.	12.
10. Porta Appia	P. San Sebastiano.	49.
11. Porta Ostiensis	P. San Paolo.	35 to the Tiber.
		4.
West bank of the Tiber:—		
12. Porta Portuensis, near to	P. Portese.	20.
13. *Porta Aurelia* [1] (or *Sancti Pancratii*) . . .	*P. San Pancrazio.*	
		24 to the Tiber.
14. *Porta Cornelia* (or *Sancti Petri*)	Destroyed (opposite Ponte S. Angelo).	9.
		16.
		381.

[1] There is some little confusion about the application of the term Porta Aurelia. It seems clear that Procopius uses it of Gate No. 14, opposite the Tomb of Hadrian (Castle of S. Angelo), and equally clear that both in earlier and in later times No. 13 was known as Aurelia. Procopius knows the latter only by its ecclesiastical name, Porta Sancti Pancratii. Either there were two Portae Aureliae, or the memory of the historian, writing as he did some thirteen years after his visit to Rome, has played him false.

537.   Between the Flaminian and the Salarian gates stood the
somewhat smaller Porta Pinciana, now closed, which was the
scene of some hot encounters during the siege. It is possible
that Procopius may have reckoned the Porta Pinciana as one of
the fourteen gates belonging to the whole circuit of the walls,
and one of the six gates on the eastern side of the Tiber that
were blocked by the enemy. In that case we must treat
the Labicana and Praenestina as one gate, which their close
proximity to one another justifies us in doing. It seems more
probable, however, that Procopius, who is generally very careful
to denote the Pincian by the term gate-let (pulis), and who
informs us that there were fourteen gates 'besides certain gate-
lets,' did not mean to reckon the Pincian among the great
gates of Rome.

Total extent of the walls   The total circuit of the walls of Aurelian and Honorius
was about twelve miles. The space blockaded by the Goths
amounted probably to about two-thirds of this circumference.

The seven Gothic camps   The camps of the barbarians were works of some solidity.
Deep fosses were dug around them: the earth dug out of the
fosse was piled on its inner face so as to make a high rampart,
and a fence of sharp stakes was inserted therein. Altogether,
as Procopius says, these Gothic camps lacked none of the
defences of a regular castle. A careful observer (Mr. Parker),
who has had the advantage of several years' residence in Rome,
considers that the traces of all these camps are still visible.
Without venturing to pronounce an opinion on a question
requiring such minute local knowledge, it will not be amiss to
place before the reader the result of his investigations. In any
event the Gothic camps must have been near the sites which he
has assigned to them.

First camp.   The first camp was placed 'within a stone's throw of the
Porta Flaminia (to the north-east), in the grounds which
formerly belonged to the villa of the Domitii[1].' This camp
was obviously required in order to obstruct the great northern
road of Rome and to threaten the gate leading to it.

[1] Which, when Mr. Parker wrote, belonged to Mr. Esmeade.

The second, probably the largest and most mportant of all, was erected in what are now the gardens of the Villa Borghese. The woods and shady coverts of this, which is one of the most beautiful of the parks surrounding the walls of Rome, make it now very difficult to get a clear view of the ground and to reconstruct in imagination the scene of so many terrible encounters. Still it is possible to behold the quickly-rising ground on which the camp was placed. 'The raised platform for the tents to stand upon ' (one of these tents was probably the royal pavilion of Witigis) 'and the cliffs around it are ' (says Mr. Parker) ' very visible.' Clearly seen from it were doubtless the high walls of the city, the Pincian gate-let, and the Pincian gardens surrounding the palace in which Belisarius dwelt.

*537.
Second camp.*

The third camp, 'concealed from view by modern walls,' says Parker, 'lay on the left hand of the Via Nomentana, about half-way (or rather less) to the ancient church of 'St. Agnes outside the walls.'

Third camp.

Rounding the sharp projecting angle of the Castra Praetoria we come to two camps, the fourth and fifth, one on the north and one on the south of the Via Tiburtina. The fifth, says Parker, 'is very near to the great church and burial-ground of St. Laurence outside the walls, from which the cliffs of it are distinctly seen.' The fourth is apparently placed by him only about a couple of hundred yards away near the Villa Santo Spirito. It may perhaps be doubted whether Parker is right in putting these two camps so near to one another.

Fourth and fifth camps.

The sixth, and last on this side of the river, is placed about half-a-mile from the south-eastern corner of the walls along the Via Praenestina.

Sixth camp.

On the other side of the Tiber the Goths built a camp to assure their hold upon the Milvian Bridge and to threaten the gates of St. Peter and St. Pancratius. We are told that it was in the Campus Neronis. It must have been therefore not far from where the Vatican palace now stands : but after the vast changes which the Popes, from the fifteenth century onwards, have made in that region, it would be futile now to

Seventh camp.

537.   look for its remains [1]. Marcias, who had by this time arrived
with the troops from Gaul, took the command of this trans-
Tiberine camp. A Gothic officer was placed in charge of each
of the other camps, Witigis having a general oversight of all
on the east of the Tiber and the particular oversight of one,
which, as has been before said, was probably that in the
Borghese gardens.

On the Roman side Belisarius himself took the command of
the portion of the wall between the Pincian gate-let and the
Salarian gate ; the part which was considered least secure, and
where the Roman opportunities for a sally were the most
inviting. The Praenestine Gate (Maggiore) was assigned to
Bessas, the Flaminia (P. del Popolo) to Constantine. The last-
named gate was blocked up with large stones (perhaps taken
from the old wall of King Servius), so that it might not be
possible for traitors to open it to the enemy. For, on account
of the close proximity of the first Gothic camp, a surprise at
this gate was considered more probable than at any other.

The building of the seven camps of the barbarians was a
temporary expedient, and when the war was over the traces of
them, except for the eye of an archaeologist, soon passed away.
Not so, however, with the next operation resorted to by the
Goths, which may be said to have influenced the social life of
Rome, and through Rome the social life of the kingdoms of
Western Europe, throughout the ten centuries which we call
the Middle Ages. This operation was the cutting of the
Aqueducts. A deed of such far-reaching importance requires to
be treated of in a chapter by itself ; nor will the reader possibly
object to turn for a little space from the tale of barbarous
battle to the story of the wise forethought of 'the Romans of
ancient days,' the builders of the mighty water-courses which
fed the Eternal City.

---

[1] I venture to differ here from Mr. Parker, who places this camp close
to the Ponte Molle and just at the foot of Monte Mario, where he thinks
remains of it are still visible.

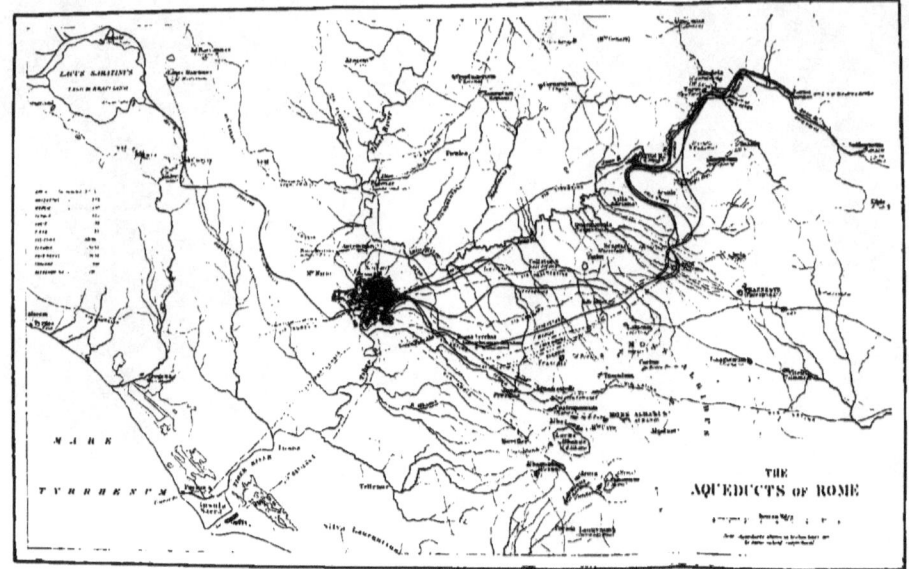

THE
AQUEDUCTS OF ROME

§ 2.—THE AQUEDUCTS OF ROME.

Authorities.

Sources :—

The chief authority for the history of the Roman Aqueducts is SEXTUS JULIUS FRONTINUS (cir. A.D. 97) in his two books *De Aquaeductibus Urbis Romae.* I have used chiefly Dederich's edition in the Bibliotheca Teubneriana (Leipzig, 1855).

Guides :—

The admirable monograph of the Commendatore *R. Lanciani*, ' Le Acque e gli Acquedotti di Roma Antica ' (Rome, 1880), has superseded the treatise of *Fabretti*, valuable as that was in its day, and will probably now be always the standard work of reference on this subject. An English student may also express his gratitude for the assistance afforded by *J. H. Parker's* volume, ' The Aqueducts ' (Oxford, 1876). The existing information on the subject is well summarised by *H. Jordan*, ' Topographie der Stadt Rom,' i. 452-480.

THE least observant visitor to Rome is awed and impressed by the ruins of the Aqueducts. As he stands on the top of the Colosseum, or as he is carried swiftly past them on the railway to Naples, he sees their long arcades stretching away in endless perspective across the monotonous Campagna, and, ignorant perhaps of the valuable service which some of them yet render to the water-supply of Rome, he is only touched and saddened by the sight of so much wasted labour, by the ever-recurring thought of the nothingness of man. But when he comes to enquire a little more closely into the history of these wonderful structures, he finds, not only that the ignorance of scientific principles to which it was once the fashion to attribute their origin, did not exist ; not only that the Popes of later days have succeeded in restoring a few of them so as to make them practically useful in quenching the thirst of the modern Roman ; but also that the aqueducts have a curious and interesting history of their own which admirably illustrates the life and progress of the great Republic. As her fortunes mounted, so

A traveller's view of the Aqueducts of Rome.

the arches rose, higher and higher. As her dominion extended, so those mighty filaments stretched further and further up into the hills. Like a hand upon the clock-face of Empire was the ever-rising level of the water-supply of Rome.

Water supply
of Rome before
the aqueducts
were built,
B.C. 754 to 312.

For four hundred and forty-two years, that is during the whole period of the Kings and for the first two centuries of the Republic, the Romans were satisfied with such water as they could obtain from the tawny Tiber; from the wells, of which there was a considerable number; from the upspringing fountains, many of which were the objects of a simple religious worship; and from the cisterns in which they collected the not very abundant rain-fall.

APPIA.
B.C. 312.

At length, in the year 312 B.C., when the Second Samnite War was verging towards its successful conclusion, the great Censor Appius Claudius bestowed upon Rome her first great road and her first aqueduct, both known through all after ages by his name [1]. He went for his water-supply seven miles along the road to Palestrina, to a spot now called La Rustica, about half way between Rome and the hills, and hence, by a circuitous underground channel more than eleven miles long, he brought the water to the city. Not till it got to the Porta Capena, one of the old gates of the city on its southern side, did it emerge into the light of day, and then it was carried along arches only for the space of sixty paces. Thus, according to our modern use of the term, it might be considered as rather a conduit than an aqueduct. It has been remarked upon as an interesting fact that Appius Claudius, the first Roman author in verse and prose, the first considerable student of Greek literature, was also the first statesman to take thought for the water-supply of Rome. And further, that he whose censorship was marked by a singular coalition between the haughtiest of the aristocracy and the lowest of the commons, and who was suspected of

---

[1] Though Appius Claudius received the whole honour of the work, Frontinus hints that he was not solely entitled to it. His colleague in the Censorship, C. Plautius, obtained the surname Venox by reason of his persistent search after *veins* of water. Finding that Appius was not taking his fair share of this work he resigned office, after he had held it eighteen months. Appius availed himself of the discoveries of Venox, and by fair means or foul clung to office till the aqueduct was finished.

aiming at the tyranny by the aid of the latter class, carried the water to that which was not only physically but socially one of the lowest quarters of Rome, the humble dwellings between the Aventine and the Caelian hills[1].

Forty years later, a much bolder enterprise in hydraulics was successfully attempted, when the stream afterwards known as the *Anio Vetus* was brought into the city by a course of 43 miles, at a level of 147 feet above the sea, or nearly 100 feet higher than the Aqua Appia [2]. The last public act of the blind old Appius Claudius (the builder of the first aqueduct) had been to adjure the Roman Senate to listen to no proposals of peace from King Pyrrhus so long as a single Epirote soldier remained on the soil of Italy. Eight years later, when the war with Pyrrhus had been triumphantly concluded, Manius Curius, the hero of that war, signalised his censorship by beginning to build the second aqueduct, the spoils won in battle from the King of Epirus furnishing the pay of the workmen engaged in the operation. He died before the work was finished, and the glory of completing it belonged to Fulvius Flaccus, created with him 'duumvir for bringing the water to Rome [3].'

ANIO VETUS, B.C. 272.

B.C. 280.

B.C. 272 to 270.

This time the hydraulic engineers went further afield for the source of their supply. They looked across the Campagna to the dim hills of Tivoli—

> 'To the green steeps whence Anio leaps
> In sheets of snow-white foam,'—

and daringly determined to bring the river Anio himself, or at least a considerable portion of his waters, to Rome. At a point about ten miles above Tivoli, near the mountain of S. Cosimato,

---

[1] 'When we remember,' says Dr. Arnold (Hist. of Rome, ii. 289), 'that this part of Rome was particularly inhabited by the poorest citizens, we may suspect that Appius wished to repay the support which he had already received from them, or to purchase its continuance for the time to come: but we shall feel unmixed pleasure in observing that the first Roman aqueduct was constructed for the benefit of the poor and of those who most needed it.'

[2] Lanciani (p. 49) gives to the Anio Vetus at its entry into Rome 45·40 metres, 'di altezza assoluta.' To the Appia (p. 40) 15 metres. It is true that this is at the *mouth* of the Appia.'

[3] 'Duumvir aquae perducendae.'

the river was tapped. The water which was drawn from it was carried through tunnels in the rock, and by a generally subterranean course, till, after a journey as before stated of forty-three miles, it entered Rome just at the level of the ground, but at a point (the Porta Maggiore) where that level was considerably higher than the place where the Appian water crept into the city.

MARCIA,
B.C. 144.

Four generations passed before any further addition was made to the water-supply of Rome. Then, after the lapse of 128 years, the Marcian water, best of all the potable waters of Rome, was introduced into the city by the first aqueduct, in the common acceptation of the term, the first channel carried visibly above ground on arches over long reaches of country. Its source was at thirty-eight miles from Rome in the upper valley of the Anio, between Tivoli and Subiaco. Here lay a tranquil pool of water emerging from a natural grotto and of a deep green colour, whence came the liquid treasure of the Marcia. The changes in the conformation of the valley make it difficult to identify the spot with certainty, but it is thought that the furthest east of three springs known as the Acque Serene is probably the famous Marcia. From a spot close to this, the Marcia-Pia aqueduct, constructed by a company in our own days, and named after Pope Pius the Ninth, now brings water to the city. The original Marcian aqueduct was built B.C. 144, two years after the close of the Third Punic War, and the work was entrusted by the Senate, not this time to a Censor, but to the Praetor Urbanus, the highest judicial officer in Rome, who bore the name of Q. Marcius Rex. The aqueduct had a course of sixty-one miles, for seven of which it was carried upon arches, and it entered the city at 176 feet above the sea-level. The cost of its construction was 180 million sesterces[1], or nearly £1,600,000 sterling, and it carried water into the lofty Capitol itself, not without some opposition on the part of the Augurs, who, after an inspection of the Sibylline books, averred that only the water of the Anio, not that of any spring adjacent to it, might be brought into the temple of Jupiter.

---

[1] 'Legimus apud Fenestellam, in hacc opera Marcio decretum sestertium milies octingenties' (Frontinus de Aquaeductibus, 7).

Only nineteen years had elapsed, but years of continued conquest, especially in the Spanish peninsula, when in B.C. 125 another aqueduct, smaller, but at a slightly higher level, was added to the water-bringers of Rome. This was the *Aqua Tepula*, thirteen miles in length, of which only six were sub-terraneous, and entering Rome at a height of 184 feet above the sea-level. Servilius Caepio and Longinus Ravilla were the Censors to whom the execution of this work was entrusted. They resorted to a new source of supply, not utilising this time either springs or streams in the Anio valley, but journeying to the foot of the conical Alban Mount (Monte Cavo), which rises to the south-east of Rome, and there wooing the waters of the tepid[1] springs which bubbled up near the site of the modern village of Grotta Ferrata.

Another century passed, the century which saw the rise of Marius, Sulla, and the mighty Julius. Absorbed in foreign war and the factions of the Forum, Rome had no leisure for great works of industry, and did not even preserve in good condition those which she already possessed. At length in the year B.C. 33, three years before the battle of Actium, M. Vipsanius Agrippa, the ablest of the ministers of Augustus, bestirred himself on behalf of the water-supply of the vastly expanded city. He restored the Appia, the Anio Vetus, and the Marcia, which had fallen into ruins, but he was not satisfied with mere reconstruction. The same hand which gave the Pantheon and its adjoining baths to the citizens of Rome gave them also two more aqueducts, the Julia (B.C. 33) and the Aqua Virgo (B.C. 19).

The *Julia* bore the name of its builder, who, himself of the plebeian Vipsanian gens, had been adopted, by reason of his marriage with the daughter of Augustus, into the high aristocratic family of the Caesars[2]. Its source was near that

---

[1] This spring still shows a temperature of 61° (Fahrenheit) when the atmosphere is only 46°. The neighbouring Julia is only 50° at the same time. S. Lanciani appears to accept the suggestion that the name Tepula is derived from this circumstance.

[2] By a somewhat singular fate, the name of Agrippa thus adopted into the Julian family is probably known most widely through *his* clients and complimentary namesakes, the two Agrippa-Herods of the Acts of the Apostles.

of the Tepula, but a little further from Rome. Apparently, in order that it might impart some of its fresh coolness to that tepid stream, its waters were first blended with it and then again divided into another channel, which flowed into Rome at an elevation four feet above the Tepula (188 feet above the sea-level). These two aqueducts, the Tepula and the Julia, are carried through the greater part of their course upon the same arcade with the Marcia.

> ' Like friends once parted,
> Grown single-hearted,
> They plied their watery tasks.'

And, as a rule, wherever in the neighbourhood of Rome the *specus* (so the mason-wrought channel is termed) of the Marcia is descried, one sees also first the Tepula and then the Julia rising above it.

This work, however, did not end Agrippa's labours for the sanitary well-being of Rome. The Julia, though twice as large as the Tepula, was still one of the smaller contributors of water to the city. Fourteen years after its introduction Agrippa brought the *Aqua Virgo* into Rome. This splendid stream, three times as large as the Julia, was exceeded in size only by the Anio Vetus and the Marcia, among the then existing Aqueducts. To obtain it he went eight miles eastward of Rome, almost to the same spot where the great Censor had gathered the Aqua Appia. The Aqua Virgo derived its name from the story that when the soldiers of Agrippa were peering about to discover some new spring, a little maid pointed out to them a streamlet, which they followed up with the spade, thus soon finding themselves in presence of an immense volume of water. This story was commemorated by a picture in a little chapel built over the fountain.

The Virgo was not, like all the more recent aqueducts, brought into Rome at a high level. In fact it was only fifteen feet higher than the Appia, as might have been expected from the nearness of origin of the two streams. Its course is perfectly well known, as it is still bringing water to Rome, and is in truth that one of all the aqueducts which shows the most continuous record of useful service from ancient to modern

times. It comes by a pretty straight course, chiefly underground, till within about two miles of Rome; then it circles
round the eastern wall of the city, winds through the Borghese
gardens, creeps by a deep cutting through the Pincian hill, and
enters Rome under what is now the Villa Medici. In old days
it was carried on to the Campus Martius and filled the baths
of its founder Agrippa, It still supplies many of the chief
fountains of the city, especially the most famous of all, the
Fountain of Trevi. When the stranger steps down in front of
the blowing Tritons and takes his cup of water from the ample
marble basin, drinking to his return to the Eternal City, he is
in truth drinking to the memory of the wise Agrippa and of the
little maid who pointed out the fountain to his legionaries.

The contribution made by Augustus himself to the water-
supply of Rome was a less worthy one than those of his son-in-
law. 'What possible reason,' says Frontinus, 'could have
induced Augustus, that most far-sighted prince, to bring the
water of the Alsietine Lake, which is also called Aqua Augusta,
to Rome, I cannot tell. It has nothing to recommend it. It is
hardly even wholesome, and it does not supply any considerable
part of the population [because of the low level at which it
enters the city]. I can only suppose that when he was constructing his Naumachia [1] he did not like to use the better class
of water to fill his lake, and therefore brought this stream,
granting all of it that he did not want himself to private persons
for watering their gardens and similar purposes. However, as
often as the bridges are under repair and there is a consequent
interruption of the regular supply, this water is used for drinking
purposes by the inhabitants of the Trans-Tiberine region.' So
far Frontinus. The work was altogether of an inglorious kind.
The quantity supplied was small, less even than that in the little
Aqua Tepula. The quality, as has been stated, was poor, the
source of supply being the turbid Lago di Martignano among
the Etrurian hills on the north-west of Rome. And though it
started at a pretty high level (680 feet above the sea), after a

ALSIETINA,
A.D. 10 (?).

---

[1] A lake in the Trans-Tiberine region for the exhibition of sea-fights
and other shows for which a large expanse of water was required.

course of a little more than twenty-two miles it entered Rome on a lower plane than all the other aqueducts, lower even than the modest Appia, only about twenty-one feet above the level of the sea.

Caligula as an aqueduct builder.

CLAUDIA and ANIO NOVUS, A.D. 33 to 52.

The frenzied great-grandson of Augustus, the terrible Caligula, side by side with all his mad prodigality did accomplish great works for the water-supply of Rome. He began, and his uncle Claudius finished, the two great aqueducts which closed the ascending series of Rome's artificial rivers, the Claudia and the Anio Novus. Thus by a singular coincidence the work which had been begun by a Claudius, the blind Censor of the fifth century of Rome, was crowned by another Claudius, not indeed a direct descendant, but a far distant scion, of the same haughty family, when the city was just entering upon her ninth century.

The two works, the Claudia and the Anio Novus, seem to have been proceeded with contemporaneously, and they travelled across the Campagna on the same stately series of arches, highest of all the arcades with whose ruins the traveller is familiar. They were, however, works of very different degrees of merit. The Claudia drew its waters from two fountains, the Caerulus and the Curtius, among the hills overhanging the Upper Anio, not many hundred yards away from the source of the Marcia[1]. And the water which it brought to the citizens of Rome was always considered second only in excellence to the Marcia itself.

The construction of the Anio Novus, on the other hand, was another of those unwise attempts of which one would have thought the hydraulic engineers of the city had had enough, to make the river Anio, that turbid and turbulent stream, minister meekly to the thirst of Rome. The water was taken out of the river itself from a higher point than the Anio Vetus, indeed four miles higher than the fountains of the Claudia, but that did not remedy the evil. The bad qualities of the Aqua Alsietina did little harm, beyond some occasional inconvenience to the

---

[1] Lanciani, who, as we have seen, identifies the source of the Marcia with the third of the Acque Serene, considers that the first and second ' Serene ' were the sources of the Claudia.

inhabitants of the Trastevere, because it lay below all the other
aqueducts. But of the thick and muddy Anio Novus, flowing
above the other streams and mixing its contributions with
theirs, like some tedious and loud-voiced talker, whenever they
were least desired, of this provoking aqueduct a wearied Imperial
water-director could only say, 'It ruins all the others[1].' The
length of its journey to the city was more than fifty-eight miles,
that of the Claudia more than forty-six, and the arcade upon
which they crossed the plain was six miles and four hundred
and ninety-one paces in length. The Anio Novus entered the
city two hundred and fourteen feet above the level of the sea,
the Claudia nine feet lower.

Thus were completed the nine great aqueducts of Rome;
the aqueducts whose resources and machinery are copiously
explained to us by the curator, Frontinus. Without troubling
the reader with the names of some doubtful or obscure additions   TRAJANA,
A.D. 109-110.
to the list, it must nevertheless be mentioned that the Emperor
Trajan, in the year 109-110, intercepted some of the streams
which fed the Sabatine Lake (Lago di Bracciano) and brought
their water to Rome. His object was to provide potable water
for the inhabitants of the Trastevere, who would only drink that
supplied to them from the Alsietine Lake in case of extreme
necessity. Trajan, however, did not fritter away the advantage
of his high fountain-head as Augustus had done, but brought his
aqueduct right over the hill of the Janiculum. Here in the days
of Procopius its stream might be seen (till Witigis intercepted it)
turning the wheels of a hundred mills. Here now its restored
waters may be seen gushing in magnificent abundance through
the three arches of Fontana on the high hill of S. Pietro in
Montorio.   ALEXANDRINA,
circa A.D. 226.

In the following century the excellent young Emperor
Alexander Severus obtained a fresh supply from the neighbourhood of the old city of Gabii [2], about four miles south-east of the
source of the Aqua Virgo. Little is known of the size or the
course of the Aqua Alexandrina, whose chief interest for us is

---

[1] 'Alias omnes perdit' (Frontinus, xiii).

[2] 'Under La Colonna, the ancient Labicum' (Parker).

TABLE OF THE AQUEDUCTS OF FRONTINUS.

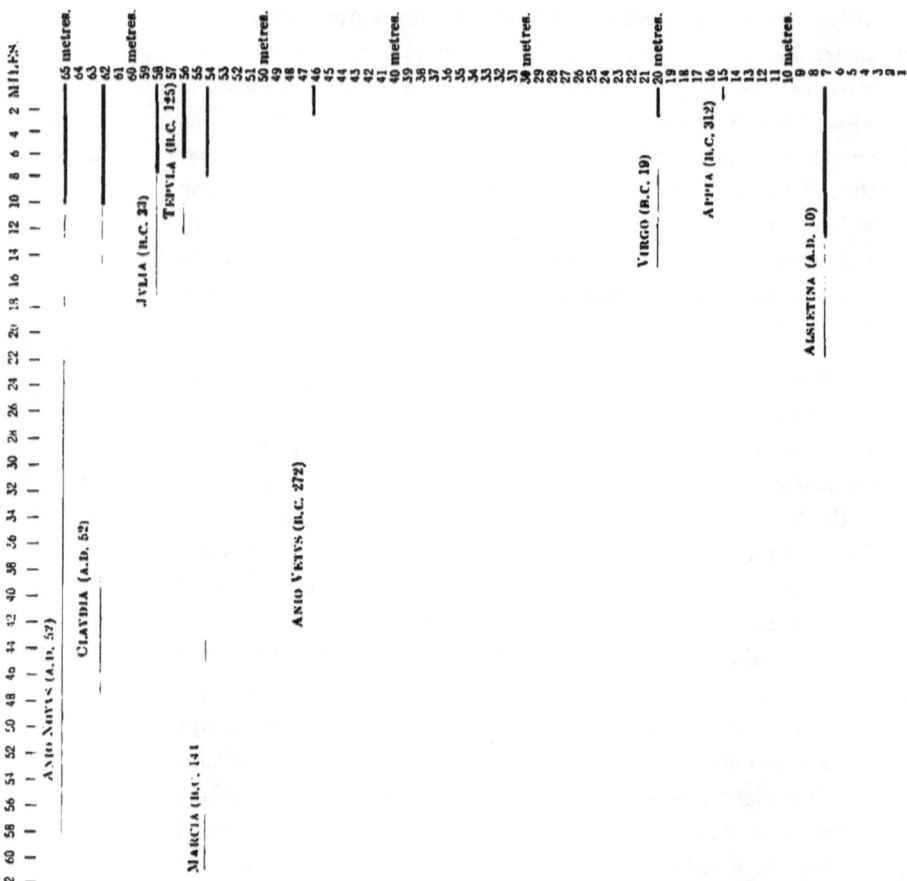

The height at which the aqueducts entered Rome is given in metres (= 39 inches); the distance traversed by them from their source in Roman miles (= 1618 yards). It will be seen that no attempt is made to represent the gradient of the aqueducts. The proportion of the course above ground is indicated by a thick line. (This is conjectural in the case of the Alsietina.)

derived from the fact that it is practically the same aqueduct which was restored by the imperious old Pope, Sixtus V, and which is now called, after the name which he bore ' in religion,' Aqua Felice. A more complete contrast is hardly presented to us by history than between the first founder and the restorer of this aqueduct, between the young, fresh, warm-hearted Emperor, only too gentle a ruler and too dutiful a son for the fierce times in which he lived, and the proud and lonely old Pope, who bent low as if in decrepitude till he had picked up the Papal Tiara, and then stood erect, just and inflexible, a terror to the world and to Rome.

With Alexander Severus the history of the aqueducts closes. In the terrible convulsions which marked the middle of the third century there was no time or money to spare for the embellishment of the city. When peace was restored Diocletian and his attendant group of Emperors were to be found at Milan, at Nicomedeia, anywhere rather than at Rome. Constantine was too much engrossed with his new capital and his new creed to have leisure for the improvement of the still Pagan city by the Tiber. And two generations after the death of Constantine the barbarians were on the sacred soil of Italy, and it was no longer a question of constructing great works, but of feebly and fearfully defending them.

The amount of careful thought and contrivance which was involved in the construction and maintenance of these mighty works can be but imperfectly estimated by us. Ventilating-shafts, or 'respirators' as they are sometimes called, were introduced at proper intervals into the subterraneous aqueducts in order to let out the imprisoned air. At every half mile or so the channel formed an angle, to break the force of the water, and a reservoir was generally placed at every such corner [1]. The land for fifteen feet on each side of the water-course was purchased from the neighbouring owners and devoted to the use of the aqueduct. Injury from other buildings and from the roots of trees was thus avoided, and the crops raised on these narrow strips of land contributed to the sustenance of the little

[1] Parker, Aqueducts, p. 71.

army of slaves employed in the maintenance of the water-way. Of these at the end of the first century there were 700, constituting two *familiae*. One *familia*, consisting of 240 men, had been formed by that indefatigable water-reformer, the Sir Hugh Myddelton of Rome, Vipsanius Agrippa, by him bequeathed to Augustus, and by Augustus to the State. The other and larger body (460 men) had been formed by Claudius when he was engaged in the construction of the two highest aqueducts, and by him were likewise presented to the State. The command of this little band of men was vested in the *Curator Aquarum*, an high officer [1], who in the imperial age was generally designated for the work of superintending the water-supply. In earlier times this work had not been assigned to any special officer, but had formed part of the functions of an Aedile or a Censor.

Reservoirs.

Outside the walls there were a certain number of reservoirs (*piscinae*), in which some of the aqueducts had the opportunity of clearing their waters by depositing the mud or sand swept into them by a sudden storm.

Inside the city there were 247 'castles of water,' heads or reservoirs constructed of masonry, in which the water was stored, and out of which the supply-pipes for the various regions of Rome were taken. For, in theory at least, no pipe might tap the channels of communication, but all must draw from some *castellum aquae*. This provision, however, was often evaded by the dishonesty of the servile watermen, who made a profit out of selling the water of the state to private

Pipes.

individuals. A vast underground labyrinth of leaden pipes, in Old Rome as in a modern city, conveyed the water to the cisterns of the different houses. The lead for this purpose was probably brought to a large extent from our own island, since we find traces of the Romans at work in the lead-mines of the Mendip Hills within six years of their conquest of Britain [2]. As Claudius was the then reigning Emperor, the cargoes of lead

[1] He had a right to the attendance of two lictors, besides an unnamed number of 'apparitors,' when he walked through the streets of Rome.

[2] See Hübner's article 'Eine Römische Annexion' in the Deutsche Rundschau, May 8, 1878.

so shipped from Britain to Rome would be usefully employed in distributing the new water-supply brought to the higher levels by the Anio Novus and Aqua Claudia. One thousand kilogrammes of these leaden pipes were sent, unchronicled, to the melting-pot five years ago by one proprietor alone [1]. But by carefully watching his opportunities, the eminent archaeologist Lanciani has succeeded in rescuing six hundred inscribed pipes from the havoc necessarily caused by all building operations in the soil intersected by them ; and these six hundred inscriptions, classed and analysed by him, throw a valuable light on the aquarian laws and customs of Imperial Rome.

It has been said that fraud was extensively practised by the slaves in the employment of the *Curator Aquarum.* It may have been some suspicion of these fraudulent practices which caused the Emperor Nerva to nominate to that high place Sextus Julius Frontinus. This man, energetic, fearless, thorough, and equally ready to grapple with the difficulties of peaceful and of warlike administration, reminds us of the best type of our own Anglo-Indian governors. For three years (A. D. 75-78) he successfully administered the affairs of the province of Britain, as the worthy successor of Cerealis, as the not unworthy predecessor of Agricola. The chief exploit that marked his tenure of office was the subjugation of the Silures, the warlike and powerful tribe who held the hills of Brecknock and Glamorgan. Twenty years later, and when he was probably past middle life, Nerva, as has been said, delegated to him the difficult task of investigating and reforming the abuses connected with the water-supply of the capital. The treatise which he composed during his curatorship is our chief authority on the subject of the Roman aqueducts. Containing many careful scientific calculations and many useful hints as to the best means of upholding those mighty structures, it is an admirable specimen of the strong, clear common-sense and faithful attention to minute detail which were the characteristics of the best specimens of Roman officials.

Appointment of Frontinus as Curator Aquarum, 97.

His previous career.

The attention of Frontinus was at once arrested by the fact that in the *commentarii* or registers of the water-office there was

[1] Prince Alessandro Torlonia (see Lanciani, p. 202).

Frontinus
grapples with
the abuses
connected
with the
water-supply.

actually a larger quantity of water accounted for than the whole amount which, according to the same books, appeared to be received from the various aqueducts. This slip on the part of the fraudulent *aquarii* caused the new Curator to take careful measurements of the water at the source of each aqueduct: and these measurements led him to the astounding result that the quantity of water entering the aqueducts was greater than the quantity *alleged* to be distributed [1] through them by nearly one half [2]. Some part of this difference might be due to unavoidable leakage along the line of the aqueducts: but far the larger part of it was due to the depredations of private persons, assisted by the corrupt connivance of the *aquarii*. When a private person had received a grant of water from the State, the proper course was for him to deposit a model of the pipe which had been conceded to him in the office of the Curator, whose servants were then directed to make an orifice of the same dimensions in the side of the reservoir, and permit the consumer to attach to it a pipe of the same size. Sometimes, however, for a bribe, the *aquarius* would make a hole of larger diameter than the concession. Sometimes, while keeping the hole of the right size, he would attach a larger pipe which would soon be filled by the pressure of the water oozing through the wall of the reservoir. Sometimes a pipe for which there was absolutely no authority at all would be introduced into the reservoir, or yet worse into the aqueduct before it reached the reservoir. Sometimes the grant of water, which was by its express terms limited to the individual for life, would by corrupt connivance, without any fresh grant, be continued to his heirs. At every point the precious liquid treasure of the State was being wasted, that the pockets of the *familia* who served the aqueduct might be filled. It was probably some rumour of this infidelity of the *aquarii* to their trust, as well as a knowledge of the lavish grants of some of the Emperors, which caused Pliny to say, a generation before the reforms of Frontinus, 'The Aqua Virgo excels all other waters to the touch, and the Aqua Marcia to the taste; but the

---

[1] *Erogatio* is the technical term for the distribution of the water.

[2] Amount measured at the sources, 24,805 quinariae: amount in the commentarii, 12,755: amount of admitted ' erogation,' 14,343. See Table A at the end of this chapter.

pleasure of both has now for long been lost to the city, through the ambition and avarice of the men who pervert the fountains of the public health for the supply of their own villas and suburban estates [1].'

These then were the abuses which the former governor of Britain and conqueror of the Silures was placed in office to reform ; and there can be little doubt that, at any rate for a time, he did reform them and restore to the people of Rome the full water-supply to which they were entitled. What was that water-supply, stated in terms with which we are familiar? What was the equivalent of the 24,805 *quinariae* which Frontinus insisted on debiting to the account of the *aquarii* at Rome! In attempting to answer this question we are at once confronted by the difficulty, that though Frontinus has given us very exact particulars as to the dimensions of the pipes employed, he has not put beyond the possibility of a doubt the *rate* at which the water flowed through them, and which may have been very different for different aqueducts.

M. Rondelet, a French scholar and engineer of the early part of this century [2], after enquiring very carefully into the subject, came to the conclusion that the value of the *quinaria* was equivalent to a service of sixty cubic metres per day. Lanciani, going minutely over the same ground, slightly alters this figure, which he turns into 63·18 cubic metres, or 13,906 gallons a day. If we may rely on this computation, the whole amount of water poured into Rome at the end of the first century by the aqueducts, before Trajan and Alexander Severus had augmented the aquarian treasures of the city by the water-courses which bore their names, was not less than 344,938,330 gallons per day. Adopting the conjecture, in which there seems some probability, that the population of Rome in its most prosperous estate reached to about a million and a half, this gives a supply of 230 gallons daily for each inhabitant.

Estimates of the total water-supply of Rome.

[1] Historia Naturalis, lib. xxxi.

[2] His translation of Frontinus, with notes and plates, was published at Paris in the year 1820.

Comparison with modern cities

In our own country at the present day the consumption of water in our large towns varies between twenty and thirty gallons per head daily, and in one or two towns does not rise above ten gallons[1]. What the supply may have been in the London of the Plantagenets and Tudors, before the great water-reform of Sir Hugh Myddelton, we have perhaps no means of estimating ; but it is stated, apparently on good authority, that ' in 1550 the inhabitants of Paris received a supply of only *one quart per day*, and nine-tenths of the people were compelled to obtain their supply direct from the Seine[2].'

Doubt as to the actual value of the unit of measure employed by the Roman water-surveyors.

The estimate of the contents of the aqueducts given above is that which has hitherto obtained most acceptance. It is right, however, to mention that a recent enquirer[3] throws some doubt on Rondelet's calculations. From some observations made by him on the diameter and the gradient of the channel of the Aqua Marcia he reduces the average velocity of the streams, and consequently the volume of water delivered by them, by more than one half. The value of the *quinaria* on this computation descends to about 6000 gallons a day, the total supply of the nine aqueducts in the time of Frontinus to 148,000,000 gallons, and the allowance per head per day to one hundred gallons. Even so, however, the Roman citizen had more than three times the amount provided for the inhabitants of our English cities by the most liberal of our own municipalities.

What share had private citizens in the water-supply ?

A reference to the tables at the end of this chapter may, however, seem to call for a yet further modification of our statement as to the aquarian privileges of the Roman. It will there be seen that of the 14,018 *quinariae* distributed, only 6182 went to private persons, while 4443 were bestowed on

---

[1] See Table in Humber's Water Supply of Cities and Towns (London, 1876), p. 86. The average for many European towns seems to be about the same as ours : for Berlin and Lyons 20 gallons daily, Paris 23 (London 29), Leghorn 30, Hamburg 33. Some of the American towns show much larger averages : Toronto 77 gallons, Buffalo 87, New York 100, Chicago 119, and Washington the extraordinarily high average of 155 gallons daily for each inhabitant.

[2] Humber, p. 3.

[3] Author of ' Brevi notizie sull' acqua pia,' quoted by Lanciani (who seems more than half convinced by him), p. 361.

public works, and no fewer than 3393 were 'erogated' in the name of Caesar, the ubiquitous all-grasping Emperor. The needful qualification is apparent rather than real   Doubtless there would be profuse expenditure, even lavish waste of water, in the vast halls of the Palatine, especially when a Vitellius or a Heliogabalus dwelt in them, squandering the wealth of the world upon his banquets. But it is pointed out by Lanciani that the splendid edifices raised by the Emperors for the delight of their subjects, the Flavian Amphitheatre, the Antonine Baths, the Forum of Trajan, and all that class of institutions with which the city was embellished at the expense of the *Fiscus,* would receive their constant supplies of water 'in the name of Caesar.' Perhaps therefore it might be asserted that there was no part of the distribution by which the *poor* citizen benefited more largely than these 3393 *quinariae* of which the Emperor was apparently the receiver.

This last consideration brings us to the question what could have been done with all this wealth of water so lavishly poured into the Eternal City. The sparkling fountains with which every open space was adorned and refreshed, the great artificial lakes, on which at the occasion of public festivals mimic navies fought and in which marine monsters sported, are in part an answer to our question. But the *Thermae,* those magnificent ranges of halls in which the poorest citizen of Rome could enjoy, free of expense, all and more than all the luxuries that we associate with our mis-named Turkish Bath, the *Thermae,* those splendid temples of health, cleanliness, and civilisation, must undoubtedly take the responsibility of the largest share in the water-consumption of Rome. We glanced a little while ago at the mighty Baths of Caracalla, able to accommodate 1600 bathers at once. Twice that number, we are told [1], could enjoy the Baths of Diocletian, those vast baths in whose central hall a large church [2] is now erected, large, but occupying a comparatively small part of the ancient building. It is true that this was the most extensive of all the Roman *Thermae* ; but the Baths of Constantine on the Quirinal, of Agrippa by the

(marginal note:) How was this vast volume of water expended?

(marginal note:) Chiefly on the baths.

[1] Olympiodorus, p. 469 (ed. Bonn).
[2] S. Maria degli Angeli.

Pantheon, of Titus and Trajan above the ruins of the Golden House of Nero, were also superb buildings, fit to be the chosen resort of the sovereign people of the world; and all (with the possible exception of the Baths of Titus) were still in use, still receiving the crystal treasures of the aqueducts, when Belisarius recovered Rome for the Roman Empire.

Gothic destruction of the aqueducts.

Now, in these first weeks of March 537, all this splendid heritage of civilisation perished as in a moment. 'The Goths having thus arranged their army destroyed all the aqueducts, so that no water might enter from them into the city[1].' The historian's statement is very clear and positive: otherwise we might be disposed to doubt whether the barbarians burrowed beneath the ground to discover and destroy the Aqua Appia, which is subterraneous till after it has entered the circuit of the walls. One would like to be informed also how they succeeded in arresting these copious streams of water without turning the Campagna itself into a morass. The waters which came from the Anio valley may perhaps have been diverted back again into that stream, but some of the others which had no river bed near them must surely have been difficult to deal with. Possibly the sickness which at a later period assailed the Gothic host may have sprung in part from the unwholesome accumulation of these stagnant waters.

Change hereby wrought in the habits of the people of Rome.

But our chief interest in the operation, an interest of regret, arises from the change which it must have wrought in the habits of the Roman people. Some faint and feeble attempts to restore the aqueducts were possibly made when the war was ended: in fact one such, accomplished by Belisarius for the

[1] Procopius De B. G. i. 19. He goes on to state that the aqueducts were fourteen in number, built of baked bricks by 'the men of old,' and of such dimensions that a man on horseback could ride through them. This last statement is an exaggeration. The specus of the Anio Novus, the highest of all the aqueducts, is only 2·70 metres, or 8 feet 9 inches high, and most of them are about 4 or 5 feet high. The number of fourteen is made up, according to Lanciani (p. 186), by the nine of Frontinus, the Trajana, the Alexandrina, and three supplemental channels, the Augusta, the Specus Octavianus, and the Specus Antonianus, which though not independent aqueducts might seem so to Procopius, as they touched the wall at different points from the main channels. Jordan (i. 479) thinks that Procopius mentioned the number fourteen from some remembrance of the fourteen regions of the city.

Aqua Trajana, is recorded in an inscription [1]. But as a whole, we may confidently state that the imperial system of aqueducts was never restored. Three in the course of ages were recovered for the City by the public spirit of her pontiffs [2], and one (the Marcia) has been added to her resources in our own days by the enterprise of a joint-stock company ; but the Rome of the Middle Ages was practically, like the Rome of the Kings, dependent for her water on a few wells and cisterns and on the mud-burdened Tiber. The Bath with all its sinful luxurious-ness, which brought it under the ban of philosophers and churchmen, but also with all its favouring influences on health, on refinement, even on clear and logical thought, the Bath which the eleven aqueducts of Rome had once replenished for a whole people, now became a forgotten dream of the past. As we look onward from the sixth century the Romans of the centuries before us will be in some respects a better people than their ancestors, more devout, less arrogant, perhaps less licentious, but they will not be so well-washed a people. And the sight of Rome, holy but dirty, will exert a very different and far less civilising influence on the nations beyond the Alps who come to worship at her shrines than would have been exerted by a Rome, Christian indeed, but also rejoicing in the undiminished treasures of her artificial streams. Should an author ever arise who shall condescend to take the History of Personal Cleanliness for his theme (and historians have some-times chosen subjects of less interest for humanity than this), he will find that one of the darkest days in his story is the day when the Gothic warriors of Witigis ruined the aqueducts of Rome.

---

[1] On an arch of the Trajana at Vicarello—

        BELISARIVS . ACQVISIVIT

        ANNOR . . . .

'Malissimo copiato' says Lanciani (p. 166), to whom I owe this inscription.

[2] The Aqua Virgo (perhaps only transiently lost), Aqua Paola (Trajana), and Aqua Felice (Alexandrina).

TABLE I. THE SCHEDULES OF FRONTINUS, SHOWING THE WASTE OF WATER IN THE AQUEDUCTS.

	1. Amount on the Registers.	2. Amount as measured at the fountain head.	3. Difference between Nos. 1 & 2.	4. Distribution (Erogatio).	5. Deficiency to be accounted for. Difference between Nos 2 and 4.
Appia . . .	841	1825	984	704	1121
Anio Vetus . .	1541	4398	2857	1610	2788
Marcia . . .	2162	4690	2528	2191 [2]	2499
Tepula . . .	400	445	45	445	..
Julia	649	1206	557	993 [3]	213
Virgo	652	2504 [1]	1852	2504	..
Alsietina . .	392	392	..	392	..
Claudia . . .	2855	4607	1752	1750*	2857
Anio Novus .	3263	4738	1475	4200*	538
				14789 —446 [23]	10016 + 446 [23]
	12755	24805	12050	14343	10462

[1] Measured near the city, at seventh milestone.
[2] 256 given to Anio Novus and Tepula. [3] 190 given to Tepula.

TABLE II. ACCOUNT OF DISTRIBUTION (EROGATIO).

	Outside the City.		Inside the City.			
	1. Caesar.	2. Private Persons.	3. Caesar.	4. Private Persons.	5. Public Purposes.	Total.
Appia . . .	..	5	151	194	354	704
†Anio Vetus .	104	404	60	490	552	1610
†Marcia . .	269	568	116	543	439	1935
Tepula . .	58	56	42	237	52 ?	445
†Julia . . .	85	121	18	196 ?	383	803
Virgo . . .	..	200	509	338	1457	2504
Alsietina . .	254 ?	138	..	..	..	392
†Claudia . .	217	439	} 779	1839	1206	5625 [4]
†Anio Novus .	731	414				
	1718	2345	1675	3837	4443	14018

[4] This does not correspond with the figures given above (* *).

† In the lines thus marked, the conjectural alterations of the text in Dederich's edition (Leipsic, 1855) have been adopted in order to make the numbers fit.

Summary:—Caesar 1718
1675
——— 3393
Private Persons . . 2345
3837
——— 6182
Public Works 4443
———
14018

All the above measurements are in *quinariae*. It is calculated that each *quinaria* represents a daily supply of 63·18 cubic metres, or 13,906 gallons.

TABLE III. DETAILED ACCOUNT OF EXPENDITURE OF WATER FOR PUBLIC PURPOSES (COLUMN 5 IN TABLE II).

	Camps.		Public Works.		Fountains (Munera).		Tanks (Lacus).		Total.
Appia . .	I	3	XIV	123	I	2	XCII	·226	354
Anio Vetus .	I	50	XIX	195	IX	88	XCIV	218 1?	551 }
								1 }
Marcia . .	IV	41	XV	41	XII	104	OXIII	253 32	439
Tepula . .	I	12	III	7	..	..	XIII	1?	51 }
									1 }
Julia . . .	III	69	X	182	III	67	XXVIII	65 51	383
Virgo . . .			XVI	1380	II	26	XXV		1457
Alsietina .	..	..	..	..	..	..	..	..	..
Claudia . } Anio Novus }	IX	104	XVIII	522	XII	99	CCXXVI	481	1206
	XIX	279	XCV	2450	XXXIX	386	DXCI	1328	4443

The Roman numerals in the inner columns show the number of public institutions on which the *quinariae* of water detailed in the other columns were bestowed. Adding these together we get 19 Castra, 95 Opera Publica, 39 Munera, and 591 Lacus. It is certain, however, that we *ought* not thus to add them except to get a mere approximate estimate of their number, as the same camp or fountain was, perhaps invariably, fed by two or even three aqueducts, that it might not be dependent on one single source of supply.

The camps are probably chiefly the great *Castra Praetoria*, but also the smaller camps of the *cohortes vigilum* and other troops quartered in the city.

The *Opera Publica* are, partly at least, the great sheets of water on which mock sea-fights and other spectacles were exhibited. We get a hint of their character from the words of Frontinus, who says that of the 1360 *quinariae* contributed by the Aqua Virgo to public works 460 went ' to the Euripus alone, to which it gave its own name' of Virgo. The name Euripus, from the channel which separates Euboea from the mainland of Greece, was given to any great artificial channel, particularly (as it seems) to a large trench which was dug along the outer circumference of the Circus Maximus, and filled with water.

The translation of *Munera* and *Lacus* is by no means certain. It is clear from the Table that the former were much larger than the latter—an average of 9 *quinariae* going to each *munus* and little more than 2 to each *lacus.* Jordan (Topographie der Stadt Rom, ii. 49-60) discusses the meaning of *lacus* at great length, and seems upon the whole to incline to the meaning which I have adopted above, and which is also that favoured by Lanciani (p. 369).

Evidently at the time of Frontinus the term *munus* was a lately introduced piece of fashionable slang, whatever was the thing which it was meant to describe. He says (iii) that he will state ' quantum publicis operibus, quantum muneribus—*ita enim cultiores appellant*—quantum lacibus . . . detur.'

www.ingramcontent.com/pod-product-compliance
Lightning Source LLC
Chambersburg PA
CBHW021233260626
47172CB00002B/743